Butterfly Kisses

Butterfly Kisses

Memories

George Crocker

George Crocker

Copyright
Butterfly Kisses 2024, by George Byron Crocker
No part of this publication may be reproduced, distributed, or transmitted in any form or by any means, including photocopy, recording or other electronic or mechanical methods, without the prior written permission of the author, except in case of brief quotation embodied in critical reviews and certain other non-commercial uses permitted by copyright law.

GIO Press Ltd

Email; georgecrocker47@gmail.com

ISBN
(Paperback) 9781777915858
(Epub) 9781777915865

Dedications

I dedicate this book to my family; life partner Nancy Sievert, daughter Suzanne Crocker, son in-law Sheldon Anthony, son Stefan Crocker, grandchildren Charlotte Crocker and Avery Anthony

I know the most important people in the world are family. You are my family and I love all of you

CONTENTS

DEDICATION		v
INTRODUCTION		ix
One	My daughter is born	1
Two	Memories	9
Three	Butterfly Sandwiches	19
Four	Activities	21
Five	Compassion	24
Six	Christmas Preparations	26
Seven	Christmas Morning	32
Eight	The Bottle of Scotch	36
Nine	The Wedding Speech	38
ABOUT THE AUTHOR		41

INTRODUCTION

This book is for my daughter Suzanne, my gift to her on her wedding day.

Suzanne was always a very independent child and grew into an independent woman. I loved her before she was born. Like most children, she had a very active imagination.

She was a child who loved to read. Her love of reading probably came from the nightly stories read to her by her mother and her dad. She is now grown into a beautiful woman and is an active duty Canadian soldier. Suzanne's great love for reading books continued into her adulthood and is still very strong today Her love of books probably contributed to her active childhood imagination.

One evening in late spring of 2023 I received a phone call from Suzanne announcing her engagement to Sheldon Anthony of Pasadena, Newfoundland. That was a happy day for her and her family. I was not surprised by the news but very happy for her. Suzanne and Sheldon had met a few years earlier and he was well liked by all of Suzanne's family,

Before long Sheldon and Suzanne were planning their wedding for June of 2024. I asked Suzanne about helping anyway I possibly could, but her independence broke through again, "no worries dad we can handle this, you will get to do what you have looked forward to for years, opening that bottle of scotch you have been keeping for the occasion and walking me down the aisle".

As the months ticked away and the big day grew nearer, I was thinking about, what to give my daughter, that would be something really personal. Then while on vacation in Hilton Head Island, South Carolina in mid April of 2024 just two months before her wedding date, I woke one night with a thought in my head. I have written and published two books, so my thought was, "you should write a book for Suzanne, a wedding gift ".

In the morning, I floated the idea to Nancy, my life partner, who immediately replied, "That is a great idea, you should, I wish my dad had done that," Thinking about the idea and then putting it into action was a whole different matter. Time was a factor and I was on vacation on Hilton Head, our favorite place to vacation. The wedding was in approximately two months, a daunting task, I thought. The more I

INTRODUCTION

thought about it, the better the idea looked. The next night, I had a restless sleep, as my thought were scattered, "I should have had this idea much sooner." I have never been a person who is intimidated by any task. The journey to write a short story for my daughter began. What is better than a special book written by her dad, for a daughter who loves to read? Here it is that story, enjoy the journey inside these pages. as much as I have writing it.

One

My daughter is born

It was soon after our son Stefan was born in 1979, Sharon and I were discussing having another child, we wanted two children, hopefully a boy and a girl, who would be close enough in age to grow up together. Jokingly, I said to Sharon, "making a boy was hardest, making a girl should be easy, I have the blueprint in front of me". So within two years Sharon was pregnant again. In July 1982, our beautiful daughter, Suzanne was born. We were so proud and happy to have a son and a daughter. Life was moving in the right direction for this young couple.

While Sharon was pregnant with Suzanne, Sharon was advised by our family doctor to get an ultrasound test performed, to check on the baby inside the womb. A week or so later we received a call from our doctor with an appointment to discuss the test results. Our family doctor informed us, that the results of ultrasound testing revealed our baby's head was enlarged and she most likely would be born "retarded." They did not say, mentally disabled — there was no political correctness in those days.

This was not good news, it was very worrisome for young parents to be. Sharon and I were very worried, as we drove home The next afternoon I said to, our young son, "Stefan, you and I have to go somewhere." We drove to Marymount, the little sanctuary in Marystown where a large statue of the Virgin Mary, the Madonna resides. This place is located on a dirt road, referred to as Tolt Road. The road was not well kept — it was full of pot holes and ruts, so it was best to drive on it with an SUV like I owned. After just three or four km driving on this road, Marymount, is just off to the left. I had been here many times.

The entrance driveway to Marymount was short but very rough to drive on. At the top of the hill, just at the end of this driveway, is an approximately fifteen meter statue of the Madonna, mother Mary, with a prayer sanctuary that is surrounded by a chain link fence and a gate that is never locked. From this point, you can see most of Marystown. The view from here is spectacular A view that includes, if my memory is true, Marystown North and South, some of Creston South and North, most of Mortier Bay, the small town of Spanish Room, and the start of narrows of Creston Inlet and Birchy Island.

I have been told Birchy Island was originally owned by the Cleal family along with land just a short distance away on the mainland of Creston South. A Cleal was one of the first settlers of Creston South. An early settler was also my great grandfather John Crocker of Bridport, Dorset county England. Birchy Island had been passed down through generations and has since been since sold. It would be many years later a descendant of that Cleal, Betty Cleal, would marry Grant Smith, a policeman from Nova Scotia, a descendent of John Crocker. Although the Cleal and Crocker descendants are now scattered across Canada and the world, there are still many with the surname Cleal and Crocker who still live in Creston South. The first Cleal came from England settling on the island and surviving through farming and fishing. Looking to the left about fifteen kilometers up Creston Inlet there is a point where it has a Y. To the left of this Y, the narrow inlet opens up into a wider area known locally as the South West. With binoculars, one can see small islands, marshes, some low-lying trees and the fresh water lake or pond, as locals refer to it, just beyond the shores of the salt water.

Most inland water areas in Newfoundland are not referred to as lakes but ponds. Although not visible, there is a river, locals refer to as,

The Main Brook. The Main Brook empties into a large body of water referred to as the, Fresh Pond. This river/brook continues on down stream to the salt water area that is referred to as the South West. There are a few very small islands scattered around the South West surrounded by jagged rocks. In the other direction , the Y of Creston inlet, continues along to an area known locally as the North West.

There are many children, including my own who have grown up on the shores of Creston Inlet, Mortier Bay. Creston Inlet was and is a great place for boating and water sports in summer. As a young boy, we would go row boating in dories with oars that were long and heavy, requiring one young boy for each oar. Scattered along the shore moored to their anchors were motor boats built by local boat builders that usually included a Make-and Break engine that were among the first technology advances to help revolutionize the fishing in Newfoundland and Labrador. That engine made an unforgettable sound as boaters and fisherman moved around the waterways., a sound that I can sill hear when I close my eyes to let my thoughts think back to days gone by. Today the sheltered inlet is used for mostly boats, sea-doos and water skiing, by locals and visitors alike.

As I understand it, the Madonna statue was erected as requested by a resident of Marystown who had moved to Montreal many years before. When this gentleman passed away, in his will, he made money and land available to erect this statue and prayer garden, later erected by his brother Tom and the Catholic Church on his behalf. On this day, over forty years ago, I drove here to pray and ask for a miracle, a favor from the Madonna, the Virgin Mary. Upon arriving I took a deep breath and scanned my eyes across the beautiful view. Stefan and I kneeled to pray. Stefan started his prayer: "God bless mommy and daddy, God bless Stefan, make him a good boy", etc. It was the prayer we taught to him at night just before bedtime. I smiled but did not interrupt him. I knew Mother Mary was aware of the reason for our prayers. I prayed to the Madonna and her son Jesus, explaining the possibility of my daughter being born with an enlarged head and possibly being mentally disabled or worse. I remember explaining to Mary that she was a mother and understood our concern. I asked her to intercede on our behalf and asked that she would ensure our child would be born as normal as could be.

Late one evening Sharon went into premature labor, with emergency lights flashing, I rushed her to the local hospital in my car, not the current recently newer hospital, but the old Burin Cottage Hospital in Ship Cove, Burin. On route to the hospital we were pulled over by a police officer who came up to my driver side window and asked why we were in such a hurry and I explained the situation. The police then said, "Okay follow me I will help get you there". Sharon and I were soon driving at high speed behind the police car with emergency lights flashing. On arrival at the hospital the officer stopped and turned waving his hand as he passed us out of the parking area saying as he passed, "you got it from here".

I hurried Sharon inside, I do not remember if I was able to acquire a wheel chair or continued with Sharon myself. After a few queries by the emergency nurse on duty, and a short wait, she was ushered into the doctor area. Sharon was soon diagnosed as being in pre-mature labor, an added worry. We were advised the baby was in breach position and could not be born in that position, more worry. In an emergency situation Sharon, along with an emergency incubator, was readied to be transferred by ambulance from the Burin Cottage Hospital to the Grace Maternity Hospital in St. John's NL with an attending nurse included in the ambulance, just in case of any further emergency situations. Later that night after dropping Stefan at his Grandfather Mitchell's house, I drove to St John's to be with her. Sharon's brother accompanied me on the drive. In the rush to get to St. John's I noticed I had forgotten to get gas. I would have to stop for gas at the only gas station on the Burin Peninsula highway at that time the other being approximately one hundred fifty kilometers away in the very small town of Goobies. I had a small amount of cash. We did not have a credit card either, but the gas station owner said, "No problem fill it up, drop by and pay on your way home". In today's world that kindness would not happen. I filled the car with gas, checked the oil and continued on my way. I did return to pay with money and gratitude, on my way home some days later. We arrived at Grace Hospital in St. John's four hours later.

I went inside to talk to my wife and find out what the immediate future had in store. Sharon was very worried, the doctors were in progress of trying to delay the birth of our baby until a better diagnoses could be achieved. After a restless sleep by worried parents, the next morning we were informed that, due to pregnancy complications, Sharon had to have a C-section, and it would be scheduled for the next morning. Doctors informed us that the surgery had to be performed to save baby and mother. It was worrisome and stressful, situation for us. Lots of prayers went to the heavens that night, prayers for Sharon and baby, said by me, other family and friends. After a restless night for both of us, the prep for her surgery began. Before going into surgery, Sharon said to me, "if you are not here when I wake up I will know things did not go well with the baby". The timing was approximately six weeks pre-mature, a lot of things could go wrong for our baby and for Sharon.

The next morning, I talked to my wife prior to her going into surgery, then headed to the father's waiting room. A father attending the birth in the surgery room was not an option I was given, considering the circumstances. In those days fathers or anybody were not allowed into the surgery area. It was thought that a C-section was not a place for a non-medical person. After a few hours, of pacing, going outside to smoke a Colts cigar, (although I was not a smoker) and lots of worry, the nurses announced the babies birth. A nurse arrived in the waiting area with our new born in her arms, wrapped in a blanket. The nurse proceeded toward me and announced baby and mom were fine. She also stated the mom was in the recovery area and would be awake in a couple of hours and I could see her at that time. Good news so far. The nurse than unwrapped our baby for my inspection, she was the most beautiful sight I had ever seen. All of her body was revealed and we had a beautiful little girl who was perfect. Her head was perfectly formed as was the rest of her tiny body. She did not have any so-called "defects" of any kind. The nurse passed her into my arms to hold. I held my little girl that morning, the baby I loved before she was born. Looking at her, my heart melted and I fell even more in love with her immediately, more love than all the waves in the worlds oceans, seas and other waterways, a love that has never changed. Our newborn had to be placed in an incubator because of her premature status, a worry for us, as we could not hold her as much as we wanted to, but she improve and continued to grow and gain weight, and mature into the beautiful woman she is today.

I believe Stefan and my prayers at Mary Mount were answered, "a miracle" was my first thought. "Thank you Mother Mary" I prayed immediately. I soon was on the telephone to Sharon's father and her siblings, many who still lived in the original family house in Marystown at the water's edge of Mortier Bay with their father.

I soon left the hospital to buy some clothes for our baby to wear. Parents at that time were not able to know the sex of the baby before it was born, so I was off to the local stores do some shopping. I drove to K-Mart on Topsail Road, the closest department store near the hospital, that would have good selection of baby cloth in stock. I purchased a set including a pink sweater, pink hat, pink dress, and a pink blanket and a few pairs of pajama's as small as I could find for my little girl.

While I was away shopping, Sharon had woken up and feared the worst, because I was not there by her side. When I arrived back to the hospital I apologized for leaving and explained I had thought it would not take as long as it did. I informed her of all the happenings. I should have stayed there at the hospital for sure, but thought I was doing the right thing at the time. It was about a week later Sharon was released from the hospital. A friend Goldie Canning came with us to help hold our baby for the long drive home. Sharon having had a C-section was very stiff and sore, we were happy to have Goldie along to help. I was driving and had to concentrate on getting us and our precious cargo home safely. All our relatives anxiously waited for our arrival back to Marystown for a home coming.

A few days after arriving home and lots of visits from relatives and friends, we were in arranging for baptism mode. Sharon arranged for the most beautiful gown a baby could have for her special day of baptism at the Catholic Church in Marystown. Many friends and relatives packed the Catholic Church to share our happy day. Our baby girl was baptized Suzanne Shawna Crocker. She was named Suzanne after one of Sharon's and my most favorite, people, Aunt Suzannah Mitchell Hannam. I also had a Suzannah in my family, my grandfathers sister my great Aunt Suzannah Crocker Hamen.

One of Sharon's sisters came to stay with us to help Sharon out and so I could go back to work, fathers did not get any time off from work for births in those days. Sharon had maternity leave.

Today that little girl Suzanne, is all grown up into a beautiful young woman and mother. She has a little girl of her own, and serves our country as a member of our Canadian military, The Royal Canadian Air Force. Suzanne is currently at the rank of Sargent. My little soldier, a member of The Canadian Air Force. She still has the pink blanket I purchased for her the day she was born. She has taken this blanket with her wherever she travels, always keeping it safe from harm. She used it as her "suck her thumb and snuggle blanket" until she grew out of her little girl years. She still has it, but does not use it as a suck her thumb snuggle blanket anymore. Although the thumb sucking has stopped, the pink blanket, her "blanky" is a little ragged now, considering the years and the wear and usage it has received.

Suzanne really is a miracle of the Madonna, the Virgin Mary of Marymount in Marystown Newfoundland. Although I did not know it at the time, this would not be my only miracle; I too would one day be a walking miracle myself as a result of a massive stroke, March 2015.

Today Suzanne has her own little miracle, her daughter, my granddaughter, Charlotte Ireland, who has her own pink blanket that I gave her shortly after she was born. She named her blanket "Peep," maybe because I would cover her head with it, then pull it away uncovering her eyes slowly saying "peep" to get her to laugh or smile. She is now ten years old. Charlotte has a wonderful imagination and so much compassion and love to give. She is so loved by all of us.

Two

Memories

My daughter Suzanne was born July 30, 1982. I want to share with you a few of my fond memories of Suzanne.

Being a dad can be tough, and there are many things that we are juggling every day. We need to hold on to these daddy-daughter memories when things get tough. These will be the memories that will remind me of what matters most.

Remember in Chapter one, the pink blanket I purchased for Suzanne? The day she was born she named it, Pink." It was a few years later, when she was about five or six, the whole family drove to Halifax Nova Scotia to visit Sharon's siblings. We returned to Newfoundland a few weeks later via ferry to Port aux Basque and stayed over night in Corner Brook to visit Sharon's aunt and uncle. Leaving 2 days later, we had a long drive ahead, 10 hours! Anybody who has undertaken a long drive with a child, know they get restless along the way. During the drive home across Newfoundland, there were the usual sleeping and the cranky times and the constant question; "when are we going to get there?"

As we neared Marystown, Suzanne in her crankiness, decided she did not want her pink anymore so she decided to toss it out the back seat window. All of a sudden there was a scream from the back seat, "my Pink!" I slammed on the brakes, brought the car to a screeching halt.

We were informed with a screaming Suzanne, from the back seat, "I lost my Pink out the window!". She was crying . Lucky for us no cars were behind us as we backed up on the highway to retrieve her blanket. With the blanket safely in the car, Suzanne was happy again and no more threats to toss her blanket out the car window ever happened again. Lesson learned.

In the early years Sharon or I, would always read a story to Stefan and Suzanne when we tucked them in bed at night. Sharon would buy a new story book most weeks during her weekly grocery outing. That new book would be read to Suzanne and Stefan that very evening when bedtime arrived. Although I do not remember the titles of all of the books, I remember a few of Suzanne's favorite's were "Jenny's Surprise Summer", "Micky and Minnie Mouse's Picnic", "Gertrude the Sea Gull Lost The Ocean" and "Bambi". After the story reading it was time for bedtime prayers and , "I love you honey," "love you dad," then "good night sleep tight, if the bed bugs bite tell them to turnover and bite your shirt", then, "see you later Alligator", and finally "good night", with butterfly kisses and tucked in.

Suzanne was destined to be a soldier at an early age. She and her best friend Mary Healy registered for Sea Cadets as soon as they were of age. Every week I would drop them off for their training class and pick them up. I usually took Mary home first. Suzanne and I, on many evenings after dropping Mary off, continued on to Tim Horton's for hot chocolate, a ginger bread person and a father daughter chat. The gingerbread cookies were named gingerbread men at that time, but she refused to call them "men," only gingerbread persons. She would say to the server, "I want a gingerbread person please, and can you put pink icing on it?" If it was available the server would add pink icing buttons. "Good for her," I said.

On Sunday morning when Suzanne was just a little girl I always listened to a radio broadcast from VOCM St. John's, through their affiliate station CHCM in Marystown, an hour of Newfoundland Irish music an hour of a mixture of jigs, reels and waltz's. Occasionally during the listening to that hour of uplifting Newfoundland Irish music, her mother and I would dance a Newfoundland Waltz. Suzanne being the little girl she was, also wanted to learn to dance with her dad. To dance the waltz she placed her little bare feet on top of mine and we danced the waltz around the living room, laughing and enjoying the special moment.

It was, at her high school graduation, an announcement was made, "graduates can dance, with a parent". "Come on dad," Suzanne said, as she headed to the dance floor with me by the hand. As the dance started I noticed all the other grads looking our way, but did not think anything of it. Suzanne had kicked of her shoes and placed her feet on top of mine like she did when she was just a little girl learning to dance the Newfoundland waltz on Sunday morning some years ago. It seems like yesterday, at just a few years old she had done the same . It was very emotional moment for me, for both of us as we danced around the floor with her fellow grads looking on. Apparently without my knowledge, this was a plan my daughter had hatched months ago. A very emotional but pleasant surprise, a memory I cherish to this day and as long as I walk this earth and beyond. I admit Suzanne a small girl at 16 years old, was not as easy on my feet and legs as she was at five or six!

The father-daughter dance is a perfect place to make lasting memories. Part of the charm of having these father-daughter moments is that you remember them fondly for years to come, as I have.

The father-daughter dance carries profound cultural and emotional significance within weddings. It serves as a symbolic transition, signifying the daughter's journey from her father's care into the world of marriage. I have looked forward to this day for what seems like a life time.

In this day and age of cell phones, crazy schedules, and societal pressures to provide financially, it can be hard for dads to find time to be with their kids. But at the end of the day, if we want to have lasting relationships with our daughters, we have to be intentional about spending time with them. A father daughter-dance provides the perfect, fun opportunity. You may not be the most excellent dancer, you may not have any interest in the latest pop music they will probably be playing at the dance, but just being there is enough.

It was in the spring of 1997 I was laid off. With no work possibilities in Newfoundland I applied for and was offered a position at the Navy Dockyard in Halifax, which I gladly accepted. The acceptance meant being away from my family for an extended period of time. While I was in Halifax I had a place to stay with Sharon's sister Veronica who was married and living there. During my absence I talked via telephone to my wife Sharon almost nightly and to Suzanne and Stefan as often as I could if they were not in bed or out with a friend.

As the spring and then summer wore on, Suzanne began to talk about plans for her upcoming sixteenth birthday and was expressing concern if I was going to be home for her big sweet sixteenth. I replied to her on a few occasions that the possibility was currently very slim but I would try my best to get there. Her mother and I told her, mom would be taking care of the necessary planning and I would ensure enough money was available to cover the cost. As the day of Suzanne's birthday approached I was thinking about how I could possibly get home for her birthday, Friday July 30th. I worked Monday to Friday eight hours a day, and being a new employee, was not entitled to any vacation pay or days off yet. Sometime during the morning of the Thursday prior to her birthday, I decided to tell my supervisor that I was planning to not be at work on the following Thursday afternoon, or Friday and maybe Monday, because I wanted to go home to Newfoundland for my daughter's sweet sixteenth birthday. His reaction surprised me as he told me, that was okay but I would not entitled to any time off with pay, but go ahead anyway.

A daughter's birthday is always special; however, turning 16 is a huge deal, as this is the year she enters womanhood. She is starting to figure out her place in the world and begins looking forward to the future. During this time, she gains more confidence and responsibilities, such as learning how to drive or working at a local business.

Many decades ago, a girl's Sweet 16 was the period when the young woman was allowed to wear makeup and a beautiful dress and make her own decisions. She gets to choose her party theme, appearance, and best friends to celebrate with her. The gathering welcomes her to the next chapter in life: adulthood. To this day, this tradition has remained

When she started school she thought she should have an allowance. We knew she did not need an allowance yet and besides, what she would use it for, she had and was given everything she needed. After a discussion between her mother and me, we decided to give her a small allowance just to let her feel more grown up with her own money. The allowance was two dollars a week. That would give her money to go to the local corner store, Spencer's, to buy candy or whatever she choose.

I also remember the day her mother was cleaning her bedroom dresser drawers, there tucked in the back corner of her drawer were a number of the two dollar bills from her weekly allowance. When queried about why she was saving her allowance. Suzanne's answered, "to buy makeup". The transition from a little girl, to independent womanhood was already under way at this very young age.

I remember Suzanne, like most little girls, was in a hurry to grow up. Her transition from a little girl to a grown up stared when she was about eight years old. One day when she came home from school I opened her book bag to check for any homework she may have to complete at home. Looking into her book bag I noticed at the bottom of her bag were crayons and on top of those was some makeup of different types, her transition from a little girl to a young woman had begun.

I prepared for the long journey home by car and ferry alone, never calling to tell anybody I was coming home. I left work, went directly to Veronica's house to collect my bag and headed out to North Sydney Cape Breton to catch the 11:30pm ferry to Port aux Basque Newfoundland. The drive to North Sydney was at least four and a half hours away. It was now almost 4:30 P M, I needed to arrive at the North Sydney Nova Scotia Marine Atlantic ferry terminal by 9 PM, at least two hours before the ferry was scheduled to depart port to secure passage across the gulf to Newfoundland. I drove the highway to the ferry terminal without any concern for speed limits. My passage on the highway was smooth and uneventful, thanks in part to the four lane divided highway across most of Nova Scotia. Along my route I stopped only for gas and a snack. I drove ignoring speed limits. I was on a mission to get home for my daughter's birthday celebration. Getting there was the only thought I had in my brain as I drove listening to my favorite bands on the CD's playing loudly in my car as I sang and tapped the steering wheel to the beat of the music. I arrived in North Sydney at 8:30pm. I was informed the ferry was not yet full, but no cabins to sleep in were available, only a dorm bunk was available, which I accepted and paid for the trip and booked the return trip back for Sunday night, to ensure my passage back to Nova Scotia to return to work, a job my family and I needed financially.

While waiting for the loading of the ferry, I went into the terminal to take a shower because I did not have time to do so before leaving Halifax. I got a shower and then some dinner at the terminal restaurant. Just as I was walking back to my car, the terminal speakers announced the ferry was ready and boarding would start in twenty minutes. As I sank into my car seat I said out loud, a prayer of thanks, for the safe drive and being in time to get the ferry across to Newfoundland, the first part of my trip back home for Suzanne's birthday. I would arrive early the next morning in Port aux Basque Newfoundland. The drive from Port aux Basques would be at least a ten hours to Marystown and my family birthday celebration for my daughter. I was going to surprise her. The ferry loaded and left port on time. After loading my car, I went directly to the ships dorm to find my bunk for the night, I was so tired. The bunk had a pillow and a blanket provided. I quickly lay down and was immediately fast asleep. In what seemed like minutes I was awakened by the ships' speakers announcing for passengers to get ready to disembark, the ship would be in port within an hour and a further announcement would be made giving the okay to return to your vehicles. I decided that was enough time for some breakfast aboard ship, so I headed to the onboard restaurant.

I disembarked from the ferry in line as was loaded aboard. I was lucky I was at the front of a line to get off. The ship's crew started to unload the line next to me first, my heart sank a little. I was hoping to get on the road first, to avoid all the traffic heading out this early morning. The first line emptied, than the crew member pointed at me to move out and away I went. I had filled my gas tank in Nova Scotia before I left the province because it was cheaper and to avoid stopping for gas on Newfoundland's busy highway from the unloading traffic. I drove onto Newfoundland with a sense of excitement, I was on home soil heading home as fast as I could with at least a ten hour drive ahead. Soon I was unto the Trans Canada heading across my home province passing as many cars possible along the way. Within an hour I had left most of the ferry traffic far behind, next stop the beautiful Humber valley, Steady Brook for gas, a Tim's coffee and a snack to go, no time to linger, I had to get home for my daughter's birthday celebration

The drive along the city of Corner Brook and the Humber Valley is stunning, a drive I always look forward to, when traveling this part of the Island. This area, along with the nearby Gross Morne National Park has to be the most beautiful part of Newfoundland. I was not going to Gross Morne today, I would pass by that exit as fast as I could heading across my island home. I had to get there for my daughter's sweet sixteen birthday. One of the most important days of her life and mine.

The weather was sunny and partly cloudy, a wonderful day driving. I turned up the music up loud and sang along as I drove, like nobody was listening. Being alone nobody was being disturbed by my singing or my voice that did not carry notes very well ha, but who cares? I was on a mission and enjoying the day driving across my beautiful island home. My planned next stop would be on the highway near the city of Grand Falls for refueling, a Pepsi and a snack, no time for full meals, then back on the road again with drink and food in my hand. "You've got to get going" was always in my thoughts. I drank in the beautiful scenery,

Mother Nature provided along my journey. I am sure, during my travels across Newfoundland, the only places I came close to adhering to speed limits were on the highway passing through Grand Falls, Gander and Clarenville, because I knew these areas that were closely watched by the police highway patrol.

My third stop was, the Irving Big Stop at Goobies, just before I would make the turn up the Burin Peninsula Highway towards Marystown and home. Goobies is a tradition stop for folks traveling to and from Marystown. I was now on my last leg of the journey home within about an hour and fifteen minutes, the final highway leg home.

As I made the turn unto the Burin Peninsula highway to home I remember a quote I had read a week or so ago: "A daughter is the happy memories of the past, the joyful moments of the present, and the hope and promise of the future".

Within an hour and twenty minutes I was looking at the "Welcome to Marystown" sign as I entered the town limits of my home town. It was time to slow down now and see the familiar sites along the road. My excitement was building, it was now about 5 PM, and I would be home in a few minutes. It had been a long stressful journey, but happy, with the knowledge I had made the right decision to get home for my only daughter's sweet sixteen birthday celebration. I had made it.

As I rounded the curve along the shoreline of Bakers Cove, my family home came into view. Just across the cove, there on the shores of Mortier Bay, in Bakers Cove, was where my daughter was celebrating or getting ready for her sweet sixteen birthday celebration. I admit I am not an emotional guy, but as my house came into view, tears filled my eyes, "I am here just in time." I turned into my own driveway. I wiped the tears with a napkin I had on my passenger seat, the remains of the snacks I had from my stops along the way. I then heard my father's voice, "big boys don't cry". Most men of my generation had been told this many times while we were young boys. My own father had passed away in 1970, when I was just thirteen years old. Dad passed while playing the according at a wedding reception. When he told me, "big boys do not cry," he most likely was repeating the same as he was told by his own parents when he was a young boy.

I composed myself before going inside. As I opened the front door, there was Sharon, place setting the table for our daughter's birthday celebration. She looked up, very surprised and asked, "where did you come from?" She dropped what she was doing and happily crossed the kitchen floor toward me as I walked toward her. We embraced each other for a long time. Then we both said almost at once, "we will have lots of time to catch up later". Sharon informed me, "Suzanne was upset because I was not home for her birthday". "Well I am here now", I stated. I asked, "Where is she?" Sharon replied, "Outside on the patio with her friends, go see her, she is going to be so surprised." The patio I had built was overlooking the ocean. Today was a warm sunny summer's day with a slight breeze. The late afternoon sun reflected on the water like dancing diamonds across Bakers Cove and out into the Bay. Just a few steps from the patio was the shore line of Mortier bay. I opened the door to our patio and there she was, my beautiful daughter. I had longed to see on her most important birthday, her sixteenth, and here I was, here she was. Her back was turned toward me as I said, "happy birthday honey". Surprised she turned toward me and ran across the patio toward me with a huge happy laugh, and open arms, with a big embrace, a few tears and kisses for each other. All was good with her world now, our world. One of her friends, a young Brenan stated, "Its amazing you drove all that way for her birthday."

Happy 16th birthday, beautiful girl! May this year be filled with joy, love, and exciting adventures. You're growing into an amazing young woman, and I can't wait to see all the incredible things you'll accomplish. Enjoy this day to the fullest!

My heartfelt and beautiful thoughts to honor my daughter
I close this chapter with a few quotes from Quora

- "A daughter is someone you laugh with, dream with, and love with all your heart."
- "A daughter may outgrow your lap but she will never outgrow your heart."
- "A daughter is one of the most beautiful gifts this world has to give"
- "Father and daughters are closest when daughters become mothers."
- "The best thing about having a daughter is having a true friend."
- "A daughter is a miracle that never ceases to be miraculous."
- "A daughter is someone you laugh with, dream with, and love with all your heart."
- "For all the things my hands have held, the best by far is you"
- 'My daughter is one of my biggest achievement."

Three

Butterfly Sandwiches

One of my favorite memories' of Suzanne is her butterfly sandwiches. In Newfoundland at the time, there was a product called Fussells Cream — it was a thick, rich cream, heat sterilized cream, with a slight caramelized flavor that is 23% fat. It is indulgent indeed. The product was canned and had a beautiful gold butterfly on the label. Suzanne liked to have this cream spread on a piece of bread. Her uncle Shawn prepared it for her on many occasions. Shawn would tell her, there was a butterfly in the can. Shawn always made a big deal about making her a butterfly sandwich. Whenever her uncle Shawn would ask her if she would like a butterfly sandwich, her usual answer was "Yes, uncle Shawn." Soon Suzanne was also asking for a butterfly sandwich made by her uncle Shawn. Shawn told her there was butterfly in the can that escaped when it was opened, He would get her to watch him slowly opening the can to watch for the butterfly. Every time he made her a Fussells Cream sandwich she would just stare intently as the can was opened to see that butterfly that must be inside, pop out. No matter how hard she tried, she never did see that butterfly. There were not any butterflies in the can of course, it was just her uncle Shawn playing a game with her. Both of them enjoyed it. I think Shawn more than her. Today, Suzanne is a grown woman and, on occasion, she still laughingly and lovingly talks about the butterfly sandwiches and how intently she watched for that butterfly to escape the can. Don't you just love kids and their imagination and their belief in possibilities. It is truly amazing, to see and enjoy. What happens to us as we become adults? Why do we lose our imagination and belief in possibilities?

Four

Activities

As a young girl, Suzanne enjoyed piano and progressed up to grade eight at The Royal Conservatory of Toronto music program when we lived in Saint John, New Brunswick, and later in Halifax, Nova Scotia. Piano training also took place in Marystown during our years living there. Two piano teachers she really liked were, Mr. Neil Power, a local musician, and her mother's Aunt Ita, a talented musician also, who has since passed. Those two are loved by all the people who know them. Both taught music from their own homes, had played in bands during their lives and also were invited to many local Newfoundland house parties where they often played impromptu jam sessions for hours at a time.

On Saturday mornings I usually took Suzanne figure skating because her mother worked at a local bank that required working on Saturday mornings, usually until early afternoon.

One memory that gives me warm feelings is at her figure skating class, especially at the end. The bird dance song and music was always played for all the kids to dance. Suzanne really loved that, she always looked forward to it. As soon as it started to play, her face would light up, she immediately looked toward me to ensure I was there and watching, which I always was. She was so happy then — great smiles and laughs. It really made her dad's heart melt and smile all at once.

Other moms and dads dropped the kids off to figure skating and disappeared, showing up when class was over. Oh, what they missed. Future Canadian Champion and Olympic medalist, Katlin Osborn, would later attend this figure skating club. She probably also did the bird dance at a young age.

Suzanne became interested and joined a Ballet training group who had classes at Saint Gabriel's Hall one evening a week. She did not become a ballerina, but she enjoyed the activity as did her mom and dad taking her to her classes in the cutest ballet outfit, staying to watch her as often as we could.

One day Suzanne heard me talk about planning a fishing trip with my friend Phil and Stefan, for the Canada Day long weekend that was coming up. As she listened she thought about asking me to take her along this time. At six years old Suzanne was not a tall or a very big girl, but she liked to prove she could do things alone, without help. She often heard her father refer to her as, "Miss Independents."

Suzanne informed her brother, "I want to go fishing with you and dad to the place you go fishing". Stefan replied. "It is too far for you to go, it's a long difficult walk and you are too little to go yet." Suzanne replied, "oh yes, I could, because dad said I can do lots of stuff other little girls can't do". She went on to say, "Dad said I am Miss Independences. That mean, I can do stuff, without anybody's help others cannot do." Stefan was not very happy with his sister's reply, thinking she could coming fishing with him and his dad. He thought, "Dad will have to spend a lot of time with Suzanne to get her there and teach her to fish." He also was thinking, "If she goes I will have to take care of her instead of fishing myself." Then he had an awesome thought, "Suzanne doesn't have any fishing gear so she can't come, dad won't take her."

The next day when her mom and I came home from work it happened. The whole family were having supper when Suzanne popped her question, 'Dad can I go fishing this weekend with you." I smiled and said, "Well, Suzanne let your mother and I think about it until tomorrow". Suzanne, clapped her hands in glee, "okay dad," she stated.

She than looked toward her brother with that look that said, "I told you so,' on her face while sticking out her tongue toward her brother when her parents were not looking. Suzanne happily finished her supper.

The next evening after her mom and I got home from work Suzanne enquired about her going fishing. I stated that "trip will be much too difficult for you my darling, but I will take you fishing to an easier place for a little girl to walk to very soon". That answer made her happy. I did take her fishing along with Stefan and friend Carey one summer's afternoon to a place just up the poll line near the back highway, a small river locals named, Hynes Brook. We fished, caught a few brook trout, built a fire, told stories and had a lunch. It was a wonderful afternoon.

As a teen in high school Suzanne loved to play volley ball. Her mother and I watched her play tournaments at her own school and followed her around to game meet ups with other schools. Volley ball, is possibly one reason why she had knee issues later in life, from sliding on the gym floors to make a play.

Five

Compassion

Suzanne being a soldier, was eventually sent on a tour with the military. Before she left for the tour she cut a corner off her blanket I gave her when she was born, to take with her. She told me it was because she wanted to take a little piece of her dad with her. That thought brings a tear to this dads eyes as I write this. If you could see the original paper I am writing on you would see the tear stains. I am a little old fashion because I write on paper prior to writing my thoughts on my laptop, it's easier for my injured brain to get my thoughts written down the way I want..

During, my three month hospital stay recovery from a massive stroke, March to early July of 2015, I received little quotes of positive thinking from Suzanne. These were just to let me know she was thinking of me and loved her dad. My plan was to add those quotes in a this book but I could not find who the authors were, if I were to add quotes they require reference to the author. Even Googling the quotes did not reveal the authors. I liked them, thanks honey. I know I have loved her even before she was born and have every moment since. During my continued recovery later at home I found a CD she gave me when she was a teenager. There's only one song on it: "Butterfly kisses." I played it for the first time in years I remembering her childhood and her growing up. Choking back my tears, I uttered the words: " Suzanne, my little girl, I love you." I copied this song to the iPod that I have in my SUV, and I listen to it often. The stroke has softened my emotions.

One day I was having a lot of pain and issues with my back after the stroke. It was painful just to bend to tie my shoes. Suzanne noticed my pain and rushed over, kneeling on the floor in front of me. She said, "Dad I can tie those". You tied my shoes many times when I was a little girl." "I sure did," I replied. Aww, a special moment. I am not sure why but it was a little embarrassing not being able to tie my own shoes and it was an emotional moment for me. I have thought about that moment many times since, and it still is as emotional for me as it was when it happened. It really was a special moment. "There you are dad," she said with a smile as she finished tying my shoes. "Let me know if you need your shoes tied again. Rest your back or even walk a while, that will help make it better." "Thank you honey, I love you," I said. "I love you too, Dad," she replied. My thought were," I must have done something right. It is the little things that mean so much ".

Six

Christmas Preparations

Christmas eve was soon upon our family. Suzanne and Stefan were making their gift list known to their parents. As usual we listened but were non-committal about any present possibilities. All the local kids looked forward to Christmas with anticipation, just like Suzanne and Stefan. At school the chatter was always about what everybody was hoping to get for Christmas. Finally the big day before Christmas day arrived, Christmas Eve. Stefan and Suzanne were sent to bed about 9:30pm and had a very difficult time getting to sleep, due to the anticipation of Santa Claus and the presents they hoped would be under their Christmas tree in the morning. After many hours of restless sleep Christmas morning finally arrived.

The family Christmas tree had its own story this year: the family lived in a two story house located on the shores of Mortier Bay, Newfoundland, Canada which once belonged to Suzanne and Stefan's Grandparents Tom and Maud. During the winter it was cold living this close to the water especially when the cold North East wind blew in the bay. It was great though, because the water in the cove froze over during the winter. Suzanne and her brother could ice skate any day they wanted when it was not snowy or stormy outside. After the snow falling on the ice stopped, the local parents and kids all got together to clear an area for the kids to skate and play.

This year the whole family were planning and preparing for the Christmas season and a visit from Santa Clause. Sharon had prepared her traditional dark fruit cake and the many types of Christmas cookies which were placed in the freezer to keep for Christmas. The Christmas delicacies would be shared with her family and any relatives that would visit during the Christmas season.

It was about two weeks before Christmas Eve on a sunny cold winter day after a light snowfall when Suzanne heard her dad ask her brother, if he wanted to go with him and their dog Barry to cut a Christmas tree in the woods on the back road. Now Suzanne was only about three years old at this time, but asked her father if she could also come along to help cut and bring home the Christmas tree. Dad smiled and said, "okay with me, go check with your mother". Suzanne asked her mom who said, "Well, if you dress up warm and put on your winter boots. It is cold and there are a few inches of light snow on the ground." Suzanne got out her pink snowsuit, her warm pink winter boots, pink woolen mittens with strings and a pink woolen hat that mom had gotten at a local craft fair just a few weeks earlier. Her mother helped her get dressed. First she pulled on her boots then placed the mittens on a string over her shoulders and across the back of your neck, the string was hidden by the snow suit. The mittens string hung down each arm to allow the mittens to be worn on the hands and not get lost when removed from her hands, which constantly happened. When the pink mittens were not on her hands they dangled on a string at her fingertips. The snow suit would cover the top of her boots, not allowing snow to get inside the boots to melt and make her feet cold.

Although her mother helped her get dressed. Suzanne was Miss Independent for her age and said, "I can do it myself". Her dad said "I know you can, but I want to get going very fast so mom is helping you just to speed things up".

Stefan got dressed quickly and soon was waiting with Barry, the dog, in the car. Suzanne was soon dressed and in the car also. Dad buckled her into the seat, next to Barry. Everyone drove off to cut a Christmas tree in the nearby woods. The smile on the children's faces was priceless. They were so excited.

In those days, people in their home town did not buy a fake tree or one on a tree lot for Christmas. They went to cut their own in one of the many wooded areas located near town.

On this day they drove to what was referred to as the back highway, a road near the forest not far from home. Dad soon found a safe place to park near a footpath that led into a wooded area near Hynes Brook. Stefan got out of the car and started into the woods, as his father was getting Suzanne out of the car. Stefan knew this area well because he and his friends had built an old camp just a little further up Hynes Brook. Dad yelled at Stefan to wait until he was ready. Barry was very excited, jumping and running around. Dad pulled on Suzanne's pink mittens and pink wool cap, then pulled on his own gloves and cap and told Stefan to pull his woolens on also. Soon they were all on their way.

Dad walked first, Suzanne followed second, and third was Stefan. Dad looked at Stefan and said "keep an eye on your sister, my son." Suzanne was just a little girl whose legs were not very long yet, so she struggled to keep up, whole Barry ran around her and jumped up licking her face showing his happiness with her being along with them. Although there was not much snow on the ground it was half way up to Suzanne's knees. The light fluffy snow made it harder for her to walk. Her father often looked back to check on her, as his heart filled with joy, pride and love for her. Dad came back to check on her and noted her mittens were not on her hands. The mittens were now dangling at her fingertips.

Suzanne was just picking up snow in her bare hands to eat it. She was so happy to be out with her brother and her father to find a Christmas tree. Suzanne's cheeks were rosy pink with the cold, sometimes the wool cap fell forward and covered her eyes, as she put her hand to push it back over her head and away from the eyes. The cold made her nose run, which it often does when outside on cold winter days. The dog licked her face once and a while and seemed to be worried about her.

Suzanne had a smile across her face that was a picture of pure happiness as she walked through the almost knee deep, very light dry snow, that had fallen. Dad offered to hold her hand but she refused. "I want to walk myself" she said. "Miss independent" dad stated. Stefan and dad slowed to walk beside her, but soon her brother was walking ahead. Barry ran to Stefan then back to Dad and Suzanne. After a while of walking so slow her father scooped up Suzanne and carried her in his arms.

Dad said, " We will need a tall tree that reaches the ceiling so we can have enough room to place all the presents from Santa Clause under it. I think you better get busy looking for a tree". Dad soon placed his little girl back to the ground on her feet. Barry stayed with her wagging his tail, as her brother and father were weaving around trees staying within ear range looking to find a suitable Christmas tree. Suzanne started looking for a tree on her own with Barry by her side. Together they found a suitable tree. Dad asked them if they thought it was a good tree, to which Suzanne and Stefan agreed. As dad was cutting the tree down Suzanne wanted to help, so dad so dad placed her hand onto the handle of the saw. Snow was falling from the tree branches as they were cutting it. The snow fell down over their head, onto their faces and down their neck causing them to giggle, as they continued to cut into the tree.

Suddenly dad stepped back and told Stefan to help his sister to finish the job. Stefan jumped in to help his sister finish cutting down the tree. The job of cutting the tree was finished by the dual team of brother and sister. Suzanne then wanted to help her brother and father drag their new found Christmas tree back to the car.

It was a slow walk back to the car, dragging the tree, with Suzanne holding and pulling on a branch of the tree. Suzanne thought she was really helping pull it along. Being siblings she and her brother argued about pulling the tree. Stefan was a little irritated about the slow progress, but dad scolded him to take his time because his sister was only little. Finally they got back to the car. Dad ensured both Suzanne and Stefan were inside the car, he then started the car and turned up the heater. After the heat was turned up and all were warmed, dad turned the heater on a lower setting. He then got out to make the tree ready to take home. He shook the tree to help remove any snow then placed the tree onto the roof of the station wagon and fastened it down. Soon they were on their way home with the family evergreen Christmas tree, with a big grin on their faces.

  Suzanne was so proud of herself for helping to find and cut the family Christmas tree this year. It was a floor to ceiling tree as usual. "We needed a big tree to have room for all of the gifts from Santa", Suzanne shouted from the back seat. "We sure do honey," her dad said.

  When the trio arrived home Suzanne and Stefan ran into the house to get their mom to come have a look at the Christmas tree they had found. Mom just loved the tree and said, "we will bring it in to decorate after your father shakes most of the snow off it, cuts it the right length and lays it on the porch to let the rest of the snow melt. We will put the tree up later after it dries off a bit." Dad got the tree ready and placed it on the porch to dry. Suzanne went to the porch many times that afternoon to check on her tree's progress of drying.

  Later that evening Dad brought the tree into the living room and placed it in front of the living room window as Suzanne and Stefan proudly looked on and supervised.

  After dad had placed the tree into its final Christmas position, Suzanne and Stefan placed their own tree ornaments on their very own Christmas tree they had cut, just before going to bed. Both children had a special tree ornament each. Hanging their ornaments was a big family production. First mom got out all the tree ornaments from storage, as they looked on with anticipation, while dad made hot chocolate for all. It was only after the family were comfortable with their hot chocolate in hand and Christmas music filling the air, did mom hand the two precious ornaments over to her children. Suzanne and Stefan were given a tree ornament at a very young age to hang on the family tree every year and always did. Placing the ornaments on the tree was a Christmas tradition, and were always the first to be hung on the tree. Stefan was first on the odd number years because he was born in 1979 and Suzanne was first the even number years because she was born in 1982. As with family tradition, this being an even number year, it was Suzanne who first placed an ornament on the tree as mom, dad and brother cheered with words of praise and encouragement, then rotated to Stefan who hung his ornament with words of encouragement and praise.

Brother and sister would continue hanging their personal ornament on the tree well into their teen years. After leaving home, their mother gave their ornaments to them to place on their own Christmas trees. Both of them still have those and now hang them on their own Christmas tree every year.

Today Suzanne has her own daughter, my granddaughter Charlotte, who has her own Christmas ornament to hang on her Christmas tree, a crystal bell her papa gave her at age two.

Seven

Christmas Morning

Christmas morning came after a night of a very restless sleep for Suzanne and Stefan. It was early morning and still dark outside as they crept down the stairs to the living room. Looking into the living room they could not contain their excitement, because they saw many presents under their Christmas tree. "Could all of this be ours?" they whispered to each other, with wide eyed imagination, amazement and glee?

The rule was, if there were lights on in any other house around the cove then they could wake their mom and dad to get their Christmas morning started Brother and sister looked out their window with hope, and noticed a few houses lights could be seen in the darkness of the early morning. around the cove, because most houses had families with children living in them. Their friends were waking up early just like them.

Stefan and Suzanne knew those children very well. It was such an exciting time. Up the stairs they ran to wake mom and dad who were still asleep. "Santa Clause has arrived" shouted Suzanne. "How could anybody sleep on Christmas morning," thought Suzanne. As their parents woke, dressed and came down stairs Suzanne and Stefan settled in a big chair to receive their gifts. As was with tradition, they both knew mom or dad would call out whose name was on the gift one at a time.

Mom wanted to cook their traditional Christmas morning breakfast of homemade toast, juice, bacon and eggs but they were too excited to wait for that, they just wanted to get their gifts immediately like all kids did on Christmas morning. Today mom and dad went directly to the Christmas tree.

. The name of the person receiving the gift and who it was from, was read out one at a time, until all gifts were removed from under the tree.

Suzanne was hoping to get a cabbage patch doll this year . She and all of her girl friends were wanting one.

As their mother called out the names on presents they received, Suzanne and her brother unwrapped them for a look. Their dad wrote down who the presents came from and what the present was. This was really great for later, to be able to remember who gave them what present. It was important to say thank you to relatives or friends for gifts received.

As the number of presents under the tree dwindled, Suzanne began to get concerned because she had not received a Cabbage Patch doll yet. Soon all the presents were open and a pile of gift wrapping paper lay scattered on the floor.

Although both children were very happy with their presents there was a hint of disappointment in Suzanne's voice because she had not received the most important thing she wanted, a Cabbage Patch doll. Her mother sensed there was something wrong. Her mother asked her if everything was okay. Suzanne replied, 'Yes mom,' not wanting to complain about her many presents. It was then that moment her mother took something from behind the tree, "I wonder who this is for", she said as she revealed the most beautifully wrapped present Suzanne had ever seen. It says "To Mary Healy" (Suzanne's best friend). Suzanne could feel the disappointment in her heart and stomach and began to cry. As tears flowed down her cheek, all of a sudden she heard her mother says "I am only joking Suzanne It reads; to Suzanne from Santa Clause". Her parents had hidden the gift deep behind the tree so Suzanne wouldn't notice it. Suzanne checked the name tag confirming "To Suzanne from Santa Clause". She quickly unwrapped the present and realized she had received her most prized Cabbage Patch doll. Her original tears of disappointment soon turned to tears of joy. For her, as a little girl, it was the happiest day of her life.

Her father and mother had searched many places to find and buy a Cabbage Patch doll , even traveling to St. John's for Christmas shopping but none were available. "The doll is sold out", was the reply from the store clerks. Suzanne's father kept checking local shops leading up to the Christmas season with no luck, until one morning he walked into Canadian Tire in Marystown, just as the store was opening and there they were, Cabbage Patch dolls just being stocked on a shelf. Dad ,looked through the names and types and immediately purchased one for his little girl Suzanne, for Christmas. It was a happy moment.

After gift opening, Mom and Dad went into the kitchen to make the family breakfast. The house was soon filled with the smell of bacon and eggs cooking on the wood and oil stove in the kitchen. The brother and sister reviewed their presents and played with any gifts they could. Stefan had received a couple of video games he wanted to try out but mom said, "not until after breakfast because, it is important to eat together as a family and give thanks for all the gifts received. Santa Clause and God have been very generous this year."

After a good breakfast prepared by mom and dad, mom placed the turkey in the oven to roast for dinner Their parents went back to bed for some more sleep but the kids settled in to enjoy their presents

Dad and mom got up about 9:30 A.M. It was time to get ready for Christmas day 11 AM mass, another Christmas tradition. Dad took Suzanne and Stefan to mass while mom prepare a huge home cooked meal referred to as Christmas Jiggs Dinner, made of a stuffed turkey slow roasted in the oven for hours from 9 A.M, salt beef that had been soaked in water overnight then boiled, with potatoes, peas pudding, carrot, turnip, parsnip and cabbage added all at once, to ensure all was cooked and ready to eat at the same time.. This meal was common in homes around Newfoundland for special occasions and Sunday dinners at 12 noon but today it would be about 1:00pm

Now Suzanne and Stefan were not interested in going to Catholic Mass or any church on Christmas morning, but it was a requirement of their mother. It was the tradition she grew up with. Mass on special days and Saturday evening or Sunday mornings every week. It was good to teach them about God and to instill some morals, mom always said. They all went to Mass on most weekends together as a family, a family time that was very important in their family life.

After mass on Christmas day, dad took them to the cemetery to visit their mother's parents grave, Nan and Papa Mitchell, just a few minutes' walk from the church parking lot. Suzanne and her brother did not understand why they did this. As they matured into adults, that memory takes on more significance, especially when they hear stories about their grandparents as told by their parents and relatives.

Eight

The Bottle of Scotch

In November of 1999, I was offered a job with Follet and Goss engineering of St. John's, to contract with CBCL Engineering in Sydney Cape Breton Nova Scotia, to manage project construction, inspection and quality assurance for a few joist remediation projects in Nova Scotia, scheduled to start in January 2000. My current job opportunities in Newfoundland were limited. I wanted a good opportunity and this was it. I accepted and was off to Cape Breton Nova Scotia on January 2nd 2000.

After arriving in Cape Breton I was hearing about a very good Scotch whisky produced by Cape Breton's own Glen Breton distillery in the town of Mabou. The thought of a good scotch was of interest to me, because I really enjoyed a good drink of Scotch whiskey.

One weekend I headed to Mabou distillery to buy a bottle of this scotch I was hearing about. Arriving at the distillery I sampled the product and loved it. Before I left to head back to my apartment in Sydney, I purchased two bottles of the aged, eight years, scotch, botted in 1999. I drank one bottle over the next couple weeks and before I had opened the second bottle I told my daughter, Suzanne, "I have a bottle of Glen Breton Scotch that I plan to keep until you are married". That was twenty four years ago and I still have the bottle of scotch today, that was waiting for my daughter wedding, but not anymore.

It was, late spring of 2023 I received a phone call from Suzanne, who was in PEI with her boyfriend Sheldon for the weekend. I heard the excited voice of my daughter, not saying "dad I was proposed to and accepted, I am getting married." No, her words were, "dad you are going to get to open that bottle of scotch you have being keeping all those years for my wedding". That was all I needed to hear I knew what had happened in PEI, a proposal from Sheldon, that was accepted. I did know about the possible proposal in advance because Sheldon being the gentleman he is had invited me to breakfast at the Chebucto Inn, Lady Hammond Grill my favorite breakfast go to, every Saturday morning, a couple of weeks prior to the planned Prince Edward Island weekend, to discuss, the proposal to my daughter. I jokingly said, "Are you sure that's what you want to do?" and off course I gave him my blessings and here we are on June 15th 2024, the wedding day. Congratulations to both of you, and may God bless you all the days of your lives.

Nine

The Wedding Speech

Suzanne my daughter; when you no longer listen or care about what I say, I am still your Dad. When you decide I am old and old fashion and want to go your own way, I am still your dad. When you think you know more than I do and when you talk back and argue, I am still your dad. When you moved away and took a piece of my heart, I was still your dad. I will always love you, still as much or more than I did that day I held your tiny self for the first time. I am your dad. I will pray for you to insure your wings are strong enough to soar. I am still your dad. I want the best for you and will always have a smile and a hug for you. I am your dad. Until my last breath I will keep carrying your love with me. I will thank God every day for the privilege of being your dad.

Only a couple years before you were born I prayed and asked God to send me an angel and he sent me you, and here we are; your dad walking my daughter, the most beautiful woman I could imagine, down the aisle to her future husband and their wedding vows, Wow!! Today I remember the first time I saw your beautiful self. I loved you long before you were born. The first time I saw you, my heart was stolen by you. That day I met you, my life changed for the better. You have an incredible way of making my heart happy. If I could give you only one thing in life, I would give you the ability to see yourself through my eyes. Only than would you realize how special you are.

My world is much better because of you.

For Suzanne and Sheldon:

I am not saying we were perfect parents, none are. We do the best we can. When we look back, there is always things that we would change, if we could, but there are no do overs.

Sometimes it feels like there are so many things in life we have no control over. During those times it is important to remember the important things; honesty, forgiveness, second chances, fresh starts, because the one constant that changes the world from a lonely place to a beautiful place is love. Love in any of its form, Love gives us hope.

To love you must care for each other, respect feelings, and share concerns. Love does not act disgracefully, it honors and love is not selfish.

John 4, verse 3-4 Everyone who loves has been born of God and knows God. Whoever does not love does not know God.

Love is patient and kind; love does not envy or boast; it is not arrogant or rude. It does not insist on its own way; it is not irritable or resentful; it does not rejoice at wrongdoing, but rejoices, with trust in each other.

Suzanne and Sheldon squeeze your wedding rings really tight and fill them with love and light. If ever you need a hug and one of you is not there, just hold it close to feel the love promised and given, on this your wedding day. I love you my daughter forever and always. God bless you both and your children all the days of your lives. As long as I walk this earth, my door and my heart will be always open for you. As long as I walk this earth, I will always be only a phone call away and will be by your side as soon as possible, and of course Mimi and I are available for babysitting always. If it is possible and I believe it is, I will watch over you and see you from our heavenly home.

My wish for you is simple to say, but not easy to do.

I pray and hope you have a full life, full of wonder, full of loving family and full of trustworthy friends and set an example for believers, in your speech, in your conduct, in love, in faith and in purity.

GEORGE CROCKER

In the years ahead may you both accomplish many goals, big dreams, learn from your mistakes, celebrate your successes, worry less about dumb stuff, accept the unchangeable, fight for what is right, wear comfy shoes, have honest conversations, meet kind people, share thoughts, find your voice and be really happy.

Congratulations, God bless you.

The Author

This book is for my daughter, Suzanne, the only girl I have loved since before she was born. My life has been much better because of you.

George, started his working career as a steel worker in the shipyards of Halifax, Nova Scotia and then later the shipyards of Marystown, Newfoundland before returning to college to complete Engineering. For twenty years George operated a small business in Halifax, Nova Scotia, Canada.

A community volunteer George served as a member of The Kinsmen club of Marystown Newfoundland, a men's fellowship service club whose prime purpose was to raise money to help kids and to improve sports and medical facilities in the community

Brain injury survivor George volunteer and served six years as the Survivor representative on the board of Brain Injury Nova Scotia. The Brain Injury Association of Nova Scotia, (BIANS). BIANS was formed to advocate for those recovering from a brain injury in the province of Nova Scotia Canada.

George has a life partner Nancy Sievert of Halifax Nova Scotia where they share a home and a life together. George has two children from a previous marriage, a son Stefan, daughter Suzanne. I also two grandchildren Charlotte and Avery

Nancy has two daughter from a previous marriage, Catlin and Olivia

George, published his first book, 'Threading The Needles of Life,' in 2017. His second book, "Let It Boil over Twice," was published in 2021. This is my third book a short story, "Butterfly Kisses,"

www.ingramcontent.com/pod-product-compliance
Lightning Source LLC
LaVergne TN
LVHW021740060526
838200LV00052B/3384